Collected Poems

Other works by Lotte Moos

Poetry:

Time to be bold
(Centreprise Trust Ltd, 1981, with the financial assistance of
the Hackney Writers' Workshop)

A Heart in Transit
(Approach Poets, 1992)

Lotte Moos

Collected Poems

Rockingham Press

Published in 1993
by
The Rockingham Press
11 Musley Lane,
Ware, Herts
SG12 7EN

British Library Cataloguing-in-Publication Data

A catalogue record for this book
is available from the British Library

ISBN 1 873468 11 3

Printed in Great Britain
by Biddles Limited,
Guildford

Printed on Recycled Paper

Supported by the **Eastern Arts** Board

Contents

New Poems

Acknowledgements

Some of the poems in the first half of this book appeared in *Time to be bold* (1981) for which thanks are due to Centreprise Trust Ltd and the Hackney Writers' Workshop, and particularly to Sue Gardener, Maggie Hewitt and Ken Worpole for their help and encouragement.   Many of these poems have since appeared in anthologies.   Other poems in the first half are from *A Heart in Transit* (1992) for which thanks are due to my friends at the Approach Poets, who meet at the Approach Tavern, 47 Approach Road, London E2, with special thanks to Jerry Brehony, who took such great trouble in the publication of that book. Thanks are also due to David Perman without whom the present book would not have come into existence.

Night and Day Poems

For my friends

Some poems are snakes. In the night
They slither under the sheet.

Others are humble, dither and fumble
Keep to the light
But stumble
Over their feet.

The snake ones whisper
Into the shell of your ear

The others trumpet
Go bumpety-bumpit
Like-it-or-lump-it
For fear
No one will listen
No one will hear.

Put out the saucer for snake to lap
A gentle inducement — not a trap

Yet, don't lock the humble ones out at night
They fumble and stumble — but they fight
Are easily, sadly, defeated.

It's when snakes and tumblers fraternally twine
You shall have your cake, eat it,
And drink your wine.

February Reflections

(Bonner Street)

Here is width, here is breadth, here is freedom
A cathedral of light flung in at the window.
Hosanna! These walls, municipal walls, will let
See the cloisters of shadow and white
Zebra-cross the settee.

Eeh, who says roistering winter is fusty, no fun?
With his bare fist
He squeezes the rusty burr of the sun,
Oozing red ketchup
Between cat's cradling trees
Freezes black-twig mascara
Round the trembling eye of the pane
Green summer leaves dulled.
— Swigging, the kitchen window, unwidowed
Licks
Orange with gin.

Tricks!
Tricks of the trade-winds rigging the seasons!
Ha, you, plum-grey, pigeon-blue
Birds that jay-walk the ceiling
Will you please jubilate here
Ere mealy mouth on the telly
Mildew the day?
      Friends! Friends!
      Untransistorised
      Distance is coming for tea

A Sceptered Isle

Here I am, a slave
Lying under a stone
They say, ever so often
Stones are turned

The gentlemen who own this island
Shriek: A monster! A freak!
Guaranteed to reek
Of sin, lust, of unbridled greed

They don't know
That with the nail of my toe
I scratch the name of FREEDOM
Into the sand

And though the rain
Washes it all away
Again and again
Such is the fruitfulness of my land
Already
The narrow rills
Fill
With the green diadem of seed

If the gentlemen knew
How they would tremble

January Afternoon

When all the skateboards have been splintered
And all the bones gone down the hill
I shall remember how we wintered
Just looking out and sitting still

Child's Supper

A cold mother. A harsh father.
The child sits at table.
— "Tell your father I've had enough"
— "Tell you mum, she'd better shut up"
The child slides under the table
      This is the way the world goes round
      Under the table, you can't hear a sound.

A cold mother. A harsh father.
Their legs are under the table.
The lino is pretty with roses bright red
But you can't pick them. The flowers are dead
      Under the table, there isn't a sound
      And nothing, nothing at all goes round.

A cold mother. A harsh father.
If only the table had a hole
One could crawl through it like a mole.
"I'm blind, I'm dumb
Please give me a crumb!"
      But under the table, there's no air and no sound
      And suddenly everything goes round.
      The child is sick under the table.

Then there is rushing
And flushing
And holding
And scolding
And slamming of doors
And scrubbing of floors
And where the roses had been before
The lino is ripped clean off the floor.
And: "Tell your mum she'd done that well" —
And: "Tell your father to go to hell" —
And, at last, disgraced, unfed,
Hungry to bed
      But father and mother have made it up
      Go to the pub.

Tree

Underneath the roots of the tree
Rough, furrowed, thrusting like claws, stranglers,
Other roots
Hidden, still formless, soft,
Are sucking in life
Their music only a murmur.

When the woodcutter comes
With his blade
And the lacerating electric saw
Will he silence the tune
Cut the last fibres?

Listen to the whispering source
It spins dialectical cobwebs
Resilient as hawsers
It weaves re-creation
Listen!

Small Change

He had the pennies of her soul
Now she's gone thrifty
Pursing her lips
He's gone shifty
Counting the tricks
Like a cat, with its tongue
In the dish on the floor
Trundling it empty towards the door

Lost Summer

No! Not already the shrivelled apple, the hard green pear
Dried, sulphured, shop-wrinkled fruit!
Where is this summer's feast?
We have been robbed.

Nothing will ripen now
Under the watery sun
Except poison.
Red, poisonous berries
Tempt stay-at-home birds.

Summer, lost like a glove
Fingers distended
We'll leave you impaled
Sodden, alone.

Oh, but how shall we stand
Each behind shutters
Winter's grey solitude
When summer gave only a lick and a promise
Shall we rue
Fruit that stayed green?

'They who desired and did not act'
Shall eat wintery stew.

Sisters?

A thingumbob stands in the door
'They sent me here to do the floor
They sent me here to do the scrubbing
Of whitewash dish and duster rubbing.

'My feet are flat
My ankles swollen
My breasts are fat
And have a hole in.

'I shall splash tears
Upon your floor
And pour my sweat
From every pore.

'From time to time
I also sit
And drink my tea
Until I split.

'Just call me granny thingumbob
— 'As long as you are satisfied
'Now I am off and to the shop
'I have got stitches in my side' —

A thingumbob leaves through the door
— How nice to have a polished floor!

Joy

Here's no tiger riding the city
In a chariot of teeth, streets blazing percussion
Just a small creature pointing a small blunt snout
Round the half-open door
And no-one mentioned, 'Come in'.

Here's no crashing of fire engines banging big bells
'Help! Let me quench this fiery passion'
Only a tangled look, given and taken
For keeps (finders are keepers)
To fill the sluice of the heart
And it leaps

Or a word, an image, jumps like a fish and whirls
                                        round the finger
Clarity opens its fan, definition unfurls between pencil and nose
And we smile: 'This is how it is'.
— Darkness recedes.

Think, how many spindles of joy
Can dance on the point of a needle
Against grim gravity's pull
— How many, O Lord, how few?

So, let's issue a proclamation
An order of preservation for you but also for me
We hereby declare, stake
The inalienable right
Of mice in the trap
To the last-ever delight
Of imponderables, token caresses, mere sleight-of-hearts
Windows hanging, on half-broken sashes, into the world
Trial balloons afloat, curled like pompoms, a second or two
Before they go Pfhh
In the air, go Pfhh
And the ashes come down.

Putting a Face to Sleep

A last redeeming pat:
There are too many threads on this old spindle
Unwind! Unwind the ransom of the years!
Here grief has struck; here folly, lack of pity, puffed,
Rage cleft. Here sorrow bruised the harebell vein
Retrieve! Retrieve!
Are there no lotions against tears?
No potion to assuage
The creeping bane?

This landscape logs too many knots of pain
The pitfalls shaded into harsher blacks.
Roll up the mat?
Or trust to candle light?
Reprieve! Reprieve!
The plough that cut these furrows
Cracks the gentle plover's shell
— Bring on the night!

To a Critic

Can you peel an egg that is raw?
Can you polish an apple without skin?
This boys lays his soul on the table
His eyes are holes begging to be filled with judgement
But not harshly.
Don't use grappling irons
Don't throw the plumb-line
To see is he out of true.
What is true is still to unfold
— Your lips, critic, are pursed
Your mouth is too small.

Debt

Now let's set ourselves up in judgement
Over the sick, the old and the poor
How dishevelled they are!
Their shoelaces trail. They fail
To fasten their door, their soul and their flies.
Like disused bunkers after the war is done
Everything, even their mouth when they snore,
Gawps, craters, gapes.

Not here! Not yet!
We still have eyes to take in colours and shapes
And the wash of evening skies.

But
The tailor's back will not straighten
His face with the needle eyes not rise
To embrace the tree's golden abundance —
The engine-driver, half blind
From driving too many thousand flinty miles,
Will not find light at the end of his broom
(He's now cleaning out station loos) —
The loom-operator's radio is blaring
— 'How are you, granny?' they cry and forget
No more threads to tie, no more knots to loose
(Though bits of the fluff still fret in her lung)
Deaf, she grows dumb.

Not here! Not yet!
We're still young
Have ears, dabble in words, in Jazz.

But
The paint-sprayer will miss the thump
Of ball on bat
Keeping what's left of his breath
Between four walls (not his) —

The pensioner licks at Thursday's afternoon stump
The alchemy of the silver pools turning to lead —
He who hid his pay-packet like a dog its bone
From her, his trouble and strife,
Now sits alone
And so for the rest of their life
Till death them unite.

No! Not here!
We're free to share
Everything: air, light, space.

What air under the belljar of poverty?
What space for the house-chained, newly un-house-trained old?
Closed in under a no-man's land's pall
They sit — or lie — by some wall
Are cold.

Not here! Not yet!
Let's slip through that net as well
Since there is no justice
As from the beginning so to the end
There is no justice
— Not yet.

But the Dogs Barked at Night

These are property-dogs
Muzzles askew
They slaver for more.

While the sun shines — their sun —
They lie like straw-dogs
Blinking a yellow eye

But when the light grows uncertain
The valleys echo the raucous:
— 'At 'em! At 'em!' —

The traveller's foot falters
Yet, from behind curtained windows
Comes a proprietorial: 'Good dog! Good dog!'

The unleashing is still to come.

Drought

Suddenly, summer struck with his flail.
Maddening, after months of slavering for a handful of warmth
We are parched, perched like birds in a cage of thirst
Tongue stuck to gum.

August is the unraveller
Pin-pointing the dead, arid, zone in the eye of the heat
Burning, turning the spit of the sun,
Rage is strutting the street.

Give us rain, give us mercy to drain clean the gully of hate!
This summer's burden was too high and too dry
A grit-mouthed, brick-coloured fellow
Dragged from between the shafts of his yellow cart,
He'll teeter, hee-haw and cry:
'The ear of the wheat is hollow; the grain must die.'

Lovers Friends Neighbours

Between the washing-lines they kissed
It was nothing, a lark, a game
He a man and she a mere kid —
No, not a game. A spark, a sharp sooty flame
Burning the dark in his heart
For her, the child
A moon, gone wild,
Turning

When she was fifteen
And her mother still beat her
He'd greet her on his way to work in the street
With a smile that meant: 'Remember?
'I am your friend'
And she swallowed her tears

Now as he stumbles past
Hawking up phlegm
To take the dog for a last dark walk
And she puts out the cat
He mumbles: 'Good night, ma'am'
— And that is that

Spendthrifts

Patient   Painstaking
                    Once a month
                    They let go
And   Moonstricken
                    Another ovule
                    Tumbles into the depth

Taking turns   Like sisters
                    They unbraid
                    Their singular gift
No overlapping   In these sedulous flanks
                    Miracle workers!
Anticipating   Great things to come
                    The balloon going up
Bearing   Who knows?
                    A myriad of dots
                    For eternity

                    Who will praise you?
Working   Silently
                In those hidden, deep mineshafts
                Who will bless your surrender
To fecundity   Still to come?
                    Ah, who will curse?

                        Ovaries!
In this, too   True artists
                Of the bodily constellation!

Woman at Fifty

At last
Love sheds
The coil, the pill
Cuts the threads
No longer staked, snared
Between auguring days
No longer scared

Though wings drag, are torn
Having borne, for too long,
For pendulous decades
The slag
Of unborn creation

Passion! — Where is passion?
Send the nightwatchman round
The knock-up man with the stick
To wish a speedy recovery
From being sick
With too much ingrown
Negation

— 'A hen is merely an egg's way
Of making another egg' —
A fowlish outlook! Born of the coop.
Here be no boilers
Stooped in the soup!

No longer to toy
Tied to the warp
Of the cloying womb
Freedom, also, has seeds
Petals — not fruitless —
Of liberation
Of joy

Entertainer

Two lines
From nose to corner of mouth
Mimic despair
Nibble conceit.
Let the foolish beware!
When he unzips the seam of his smile
It's not to bare
His ravenous appetites
The lips merely twitch
Tongue unseen.

His eyes may be raisins
Stewed in black innocence
But they leak.
Tears of malice
Are skewered on toothpicks, adroitly,
Before they can sting
Before they can smart
Before they can risk the heart.

Yet the voice — flat but scuffed
As a skittle-alley —
Gives the showman, the man-show, away.
Let his feet dance quadrilles
Let his hands flutter — candles adrift,
Snuffed by every draught —
We know his heart is not in his guts
And are tinnily grateful
To be seduced so lightly.

George and the Vulture

I'll tell you a story you never heard tell
Of George, the hero, and his wee bird as well
That'd eat out of his hand and prettily coo
And the band round its neck was red, white and blue
'Righto', says Georgie, 'that bird will do'.
   Chorus: For the band round its neck was red, white and blue.

Oh, Georgie-Porgie, you silly old cove!
That bird is a vulture. That isn't a dove
It will rip you and trick you and bite off your ... 'O no',
Cries Georgie, 'let's give it a toe'
   Chorus: 'No, no', cries Georgie, 'I'll give it a toe'.

Poor old Georgie no longer can stand.
That's just the beginning. But the end is at hand
For that greedy vulture will, bit by bit, eat
His fingers, his tootsies, and most of his feet
And drop them like chips over Threadneedle Street!
   Chorus: Three cheers for Blue Chips in Threadneedle Street!

Oh, you good people, it grieves me to tell
Georgie's half-gone but the vulture is 'swell'.
It dines in the City on oyster-pudding and wine
At 16% Base Rate that vulture does fine.
   Chorus: At 16% the vultures do fine. *

Now all you good citizens, do mark my words
Look at their beaks before feeding sleek birds!
For if I have told this story in vain
I'll have to tell it all over again.

* WARNING: Interest rates can go up as well as down.

Sea-Change   Encompassed

Keep away from the seducer's
Angling, tangling, hungering eyes.
Depth-charge kisses will reduce you
To a hung-up, dangling bride.

Oh, they strain, and, oh, they hanker!
Let them thresh! For, in truth, they ride at anchor
Tied — the chain is made of flesh —
To some mum or wifely thumb
      Or they wouldn't be so fresh
      Or so glum.

Keep away from softly floating, water-baby, snorkelled rakes
And their fearful, tearful, doting, longitudinal mistakes.

Sparrow Visiting

Melancholy writes a poem at night
It comes on furtive wings
On furtive wings it flies.
Hold out your hand, let it settle like a bird.

Peck, little bird, unhusk hazardous dreams

Leapfrogging into verse.

Eagles, treading tragedy,
Tearing open yesterday's scars,
Drink bile
But you — slight, sad poem, beating uncertain wings —
I can hold in the hollow of my hand
With only one grain of love
And no wisdom.

26

Having an Affair with
a Foreign Language

Like living with a mistress — not your wife —
You kiss as through a veil, as through a mist
As you never have kissed before in your life
Trespassing on another's delights.

You have no rights:
If you are timid, dense or uninspired
She'll be tense, pretend to be tired,
If, fired by her inexhaustible charms,
You take her boldly in your arms
She'll show you coldly to the door:
— 'I don't think we've met before' —

The stars do not fade, the sun never rises
Without some unforeseeable teaser or crisis
A feast of joy
A sodden fall
A sudden coming to grief
And as you toy
And as you uncover
Her intricate beauty fold by fold
You sigh with relief:
At least,
I'm only her lover
Not everything needs to be told.

We Let 'Em Out Sooner Now

Cheeseparing!
Knife into bone!
Straight to the marrow!

We let 'em out sooner now

Shrivelled black peppercorns someone forgot to grind small
They sprinkle pavements, seats, benches, anything public,
Sit
Frightening
Frightened
Or try, from under a thin crust of 'authorized' tablets,
A soft-mannered smile
— To please.

We get 'em out sooner now

Hence the muttering across the table
Fingers twisting, round invisible reels, invisible threads,
Hence the curses; prayers, held in a jelly of tears;
Gobbets of thought, unchoked,
Hurled at the air.

We make 'em go sooner now

Hence the steps — foot up-foot down —
Which way? — That way — faltering.
A gavotte of schizophrenia
Dances the street.

We push 'em out sooner now

On the jagged teeth of a 'Caring Society'
CARING FOR WHAT?
Back on the wheel that broke them before

The clenched family wrath
They had fled.

Cheeseparing!
Knife into bone!
To the marrow!

Trees — you listen!
Stones — do not turn a deaf ear!
Clouds — weep!
         Man is leaching man's heart.

Goose Girl

She moves in a cloud of decision
In a whirlwind of Left and Right
The dividing rod twigs to her vision
Yet she's as light as a sprite.

She rules, with a switch of iron,
Her flock. Though she knows
Come St. Martin, most will be killed
But she's the one to rely on
The rock on which churches are built.

O little maid persevering
Mind, not to grow horny feet
For, comes the season of plucking and shearing,
You too may be hung up and be ate.

The Black Shawl

After a visit to Portugal

He who could pierce my grief
Has gone
Ogling, in foreign cities
Flesh he mustn't buy
For he is the provider
His scrapings the seedcorn
I peck.

Poverty has honed
My five-foot-two body
Yet even a small house
May be empty
And only the North wind
Enters
Rattling the door.

He whose arms were my house
Sleeps, unhoused,
Underneath big cities
Scraping a living
As though dead
Even a dog must eat!
       — Let the black shawl of sorrow
        Cover all!

Servants Dancing

i.m. Portugal, 1975

In the evening
The servants come down to the beach
Play, swim in the sea
What makes them leap in the dusk-filled air?
What spring releases their tired limbs
As though testing for things
Still to be?

The ship-shape big house
Stands back, sealed off, wrapped
— As in sailcloth white —
In its surfeit of leisure
But the laughter is here:
The poor shall inherit the sand
At night.

O Lord, give us all
Such another soft, gentle night
So we, too, may understand
Call answering call
Hand reaching for hand
Across the impenitent wall.

Algarve five a.m.

In the east — a ravening sun raking the sky
In the west — the moon, dying a slaked, pale, elegant death
In the east — red, fiery breath, racing over the quickening sand
In the west — white moon drawing us on — like a tide.

Now trees, still damp, trawled from the night's knife-blue hand,
Swim through flickers of light into the hesitant crescent of day.
Sway. Lay bands of undulent shade, still hazy, still vague,
On the wild, red, unsmoothable clay
— The red, Moorish, untameable land.

If you think

If you think
Blows
Struck in Ireland
Won't hurt you
Think again
They will hurt you.
If you think
The knife
Slid between the ribs of a Pakistani
Will glance off your lighter skin
Think again.

If you think
Bullets hissing towards beating hearts
In some country we know nothing about
Will miss you
Think again
They will not miss your beating heart.

If you think
Needles
Jabbed into veins
To make the blood run docile
Won't prick you
Think again.

They will hurt you, hit you, prick you
And they will not miss you.
We are all one
One trembling human flesh.

Making Fish Soup in the Sea of Tarshish

Listen, Jonah, old boy, what makes you so sure you are safe,
                                      never mind, saved?
Just because Nineveh, the fat cat, the old whore,
                                  having last flings at last things
Is tonguing her last-ever chop-chop
While you piddle in fishy neutrality?

Isn't it time though (Think, Jonah, think!)
You un-whaled, point-blank, knife-point-blank,
To do your bit of agitation and propaganda — as programmed?

I've got news for you, Jonah, intrepid squatter,
The fish you inhabit is sick, about to kick a million-ton bucket.
What you thought was zig-zag maritime progress
Are death-throes.

Up to you, Jonah, timorous prophet,
To draw your conclusions
And knife.

The Road

We are searching for a city
We don't know
Thirsting for a river
That may, or may not, flow.
The signposts have crashed
The milestones been smashed
Under the circling buzzard's eye.
O my brothers and sisters
Do not cry.

At which turning
Which burning bush, spurning its own slow glow,
Did we go wrong?
How long, O Lord, how long
Amidst these thorns, these naked wrinkled stones
Must we go on?
O my brothers and sisters
Have pity on your bones.

This road is the only city
We shall ever know.

Guest Workers

Hunger pushes
Eating attracts.
Here they come with their bundles and sacks
Run — rejects flung from the railway track —
Towards the exits
      Where no one expects,

Sell their cheap sweat to the harshest buyer,
Are hasped like pieces of string,
Clasped to the burning breast of a Djinn, a moloch of fire,
                      turning huge arms,
Drinking iron but thirsting for flesh
      No one protects

And still they come
To lend shadow-lives to a shadow-land's power,
To discard or to kill
Or scrape off like slag when the firing is done
When the cooling-tower and the chimney-stack's long
                    black tongue have gone dead
And the slapping belt in the shed where they had spun
Hangs slack, has gone dumb.
      Now let the strangers go back,

Back with their cartons and battery-sets
Back to the fissured earth, the sun-crusted slum they had fled.
No one owes them a debt,
No one owes them a crumb
Of bread.

Lost Letter Found

This was the fence that, even broken, cracked
                Had hatched her in
                                Then let her run. But not escape.

Flecked like the back of an old woman's hand
                                  This letter, tugging at her heart

Tangled pursuant through the undergrowth of youth
                — How many greener, harder years away?
                            So shrunk! Such easy game!

Willing her, in silent supplication
                        To re-invent a new-found balance

Staking no claim, save:
                        'Please send some cotton thread!' —
Instead of
                Yet another-stone-for bread - to hide
                    In wilful arabesques
                            What must not be said,

Like: 'I have no bread. I live on charity. Alone.'

Or this: 'Address? At wit's end. Nose just above water.
                              Feet stuck in sand' —

Blind grit
                Of defeat and shame, thrown against broken pane
                          From empty hand

Letter not answered
                      She did, maybe, forget

Too slowly shed
                Old bitterness, cocooned in unresolved regret
                Now bled — as from a fresh-cut wound.

As to the cotton-thread (She did not send)
                    Who needs this to be told?

Her daughters laugh:
        Their mother, stranger in a borrowed land,
                    Their mother, too, is old.

Scapegoat

The scapegoat lifts its rugged head
And bleats into the fearful air:
'Have pity, you whose name is fair
With one condemned to graze your shame

The beasts of prey are drawing near
Help me! — You who are, as yet, not dead

Or did you think
By staking me
You would escape?
And did you think
My being slain
Would let you live?

Beyond Lewisham

London, soiled Cinderella, sits on dank, southernmost shanks
Dishevelled amidst ashes no pigeon will pick
What's there to pick — or to nick — at New Cross Station
But new crosses for old?

Not to rip open each other's throat
Not to tip, from torn flanks, passengers on to a last
                                        quickie death-trip
Trains shunt, slant, recant — back to the unlit bank
Of a station long gone defunct

Past unspeakable abomination
Past the past's non-deliverance,
Desolation held fast in a splint of encrusted,
                                 rusted, scrap-iron cast.

When, at last, there's acceleration
Towards a facade of trees, thin gardens let out —
                         like little old men — to air,
Houses, doubly-detached, clutching each other's
                      looped, antennaed, steel hair.

Now stations are growing polite, names inscribed
                          on luminous white
Implying, to travellers' eyes, intimations of 'Park' and 'Grove'
Where stove-black gates will retract, playing at
                      catch-the-train tack

But, alas, even in property-owning Bromley
                    the police must contain
Unlicensed licence: flickering, funk-holing punk
                   high on an unending scream
'Steamers', driven by hidden, deep steam.

How long before gentility cracks?

Before guards have to protect gated stations
                              from being wrecked?
— This is the end of the line: An umbilical cord
                              that had better be snapped

For, just up a few miles, breathing down necks,
Lewisham waits and expects
Will there be time to retract?

Will there be time
For innocent you and me
To have honey for tea?

Stricken City

'If there were many it wasn' t I'
       Oedipus Rex addressing the stricken City

'If there were many it wasn't I,
Not I committing the deed
Let the witnesses speak!' —
Ten thousand stand numb
Seemingly, seeingly, dumb.

If there were many
Each I is absolved
Horror resolved
In a shrug, even a smile:
'You know how it was. You know how it is.'

Innocents all .. Yet they persist
Holding on to their gain
In every pocket sits a fist
— The stricken City
Is to be struck again.

For Dylan Thomas

Spellbinder spilt
Scuffling young hound, truffle-nose snuffling for rhymes
That will unpurse parsing mean lips
Goat-in-the-door shuffler of unlicensed lines
You've led us on, young brother,
Don Juan of honeyed slips of the tongue,
To smother our uncertain swords
In the silt, the lime, the lilt
of curlicued words
THAT WILL NOT SERVE.

Dead young drunkard,
'The force that through the green fuse drives ...'
De-fused, at long last, burnt too dry
To wet the whistle
That blew the hunchback-flasher in the park
Or the child, defiled by war, cast into a dark tomb,
Or old men, lives sorted out by a bomb
Into flesh, gore and gristle.

Your appleyards — under a blue-for-a-baby-boy sky —
Stayed green, would not wax golden,
Hitched to a waning pall-for-a-poet itinerant star
But how beholden we are to the wastrel,
Swilling and spilling his driven time,
For never a rhyme was lost
But tossed, Shrove-Tuesday panned, double-dotted and punned
Ash-Wednesday-shriven and cindered
Let and unhindered and scanned

And slotted, plotted — the lot
Heaving, speeding and teasing
Even our own scant crop
Not to stray — but to plop
Into its clotted crab-apple pot

— Against a needy, wintry day.

The Just

For S.

'I pondered all these things, and how men fight and lost the battle, and the thing they fought for comes in spite of their defeat, and when it comes turns out not to be what they meant, and other men have to fight for what they meant under another name.'

William Morris

Every so often
In each generation
Some one will wake with a smile:
'I who've learned to expect nothing
Will, henceforth, expect a great many things
A great many great things
Myself included
The world included
True' — and here follows a list of shortcomings —
'But, from now on, no sparrow shall fall
No neck be bent, no song be stifled
But I shall try
To break the fall, right the declivity, unlock the silence
With others, my comrades, my brothers
Until breath leaves us' —

And breath did indeed leave them

Every so often
In each generation
Some one will wake with a smile

Middle-Aged Lover

Pliant
A stew much stirred
Not a little burnt
He has turned
In blurred, blunted defiance
Into a handyman
A taker of care
In a vacant place

An also-ran
Whose pillow in the big bed is shunted
When he's out of the way
Yet, when an early ray slanted
On his tendered grey face
He still was her man

Only the stairs
Know
How heavy, how slow
His feet
Come and go

Last Rites

*(Remembering a black youth who 'shot himself' in the entrance
to Stoke Newington police station)*

The Law is not for you, brother
The Law is not for us
It sits and nods where it belongs:
The Court of the rich
They decide — the infallible gods —
Which is which and what's what
And who dies
Of homo- or sui-cide
— And bury the dead under perjury's dust.

The Law is not for you, brother
The Law is not for us
At the inquest that would not quest
They who'd tied death like a hawk to their wrist
Knew best whose was the finger, whose was the fist
And, to wipe out the trace,
Shoved sand on your broken face.

The Law is not for you, brother
The Law is not for us
And when the gun, dark eye of death,
Stared in on your tongue and stifled your cry
Even then
Twelve good men and true
Washed our boys, our brave boys, whiter than blue.

— But little black boy
Did not talk back.

Jailbird is Dead

i.m. A. Gramsci

Jailbird is dead — at last
He died on a bed of rough-cast stones
But, before he breathed his last,
There came the voices: 'We want the bones'.

We want the eyes that no longer can see,
Give us the tongue now it can't disagree,
We claim the throat, emptied of song.
That song was too loud.   Went on too long.

Bare bones travelled the continents,
Vice-Presidents paid 'em compliments,
Even the Pope fluttered a smile,
Dimpled in bile.

And what did little jailbird sing
That made his jailers murder him?
Pack a small suitcase and ask at the jail
And they will tell you — without fail.

Couple

This couple is
Are
Like an apple
And its worm
Which is the apple?
Which the worm?
— Each has its turn

Too late too soon

September twangs an end to resolution
The swollen seeds must fall
Into their wintry rest
To map another, far-off, season's net
Tenacity is all. And fruitfulness not yet.

Like birds that sit waiting
For their hard-shelled duds to crack
We wait for floods
To rid us of the dead, anchored
Like heavy, late, unwanted guests.

The gaudy month will not reprieve
What was undone and left abandoned.
Released from narrow nests
We land — all aim and swiftness gone —
At random

Till grey November, drawing in its mists,
Will screen the summer's wanton blunders
And we shall drift — like seagulls driven inland
                              by the frost —
Into regretting what, too well remembered,
                              has been lost:
A foolish summer's futile gifts.

Here comes Hedgehog

Here comes hedgehog
Do not tickle!
For every dream he ever spilled
He has willed another prickle,
With every joy he's spoiled and killed
He feels more securely quilled.

Not for him metamorphosis
Of pupa into butterfly
Here's metamorphosis in reverse:
From bubbling, troubling youth-neurosis
— Soon denied —
To: Down to earth and snout applied!

And spying aught that sings and flies
He smirks and sighs: 'You, too, my friend will come to terms
Eating worms' —

As to love
With so much prickle
How would one know
Who is above, and who below?

Here comes hedgehog
Do not tickle!
For everything he ever liked
He has spiked.

But, look, his little snout is pink
He may not love — but he can drink.

Guard Dogs of Liberty

*'German guard-dogs are guarding an old, defunct, Jewish
cemetery in London, E9'*

Unleashed, they're bold
Unmuzzled, they know, even untold,
You and me
Have no territory
— No, not even that of the dead —
To hold or defend.
They watch for the knee that won't bend
They go for the throat
Each tooth is proof of their being free.
They'll teach us the truth
About Liberty
— Their Liberty.

Not now but soon

Not now
But soon
But in a second
Second eats second

As a film though hasped, reels to its end
Unravelled sum of negations, of slits, of gaps
Till, uncradled, it snaps
And projections, no longer homing,
Flicker and lapse.

Here I sit, pushing word after word through a gap
                              in the future
(Not yet. But soon. In a second, a decade
                         a fractured century broken)
Leaving my spoor
Tending to signals.

White Day in a Black Season

Today shall unfold like a sheet
You and me holding one side
White, innocent — freed
From black graffiti's crows-feet

Today, only the distant grief
And blight lying like dust
Like dust lying light
Flying high — as thistledown seed

Today we shall eat
And smile
And write milk-white red rhymes
A hymn to the chink
In this spring's
Iron-clad skies

Elephant Wings   (How now?)

Elephant wings whirr through the air
Here comes Ms. Hubbard, whose cupboard is bare.
Keats is coming for dinner, you humble maid,
Clare wants his breakfast — table laid.
You scrimp and you scrape: one egg on each plate.
Shelley, as usual, is being late.

Who'll scrub the porch for such giant feet?
Who'll hold a candle east of Liverpool Street?

Short-Distance Runner

Cutting loose from the pat-a-cake pap, the tender noose of
spoon-fed love
She ran
(Her mother found shoes, two little boats, points of no-return
by the gate)
Ran, lured by the night's moon-fed, sardonic bait
Where the almost wild animals lie in wait:
The sweaty bull; the hissing, spitting, noctivagant cat;
and the jabbering ape

Who called her 'soft' yet drove her hard with resentment's
bent stick,
Didn't forget — or forgive —
The house with white blinds and 'No-Trespassers!' signs
She'd left behind and wouldn't regret,

Thus setting at nought their own desolate choice:
NOT TO BELONG
While she took the freedom they'd bought at a bitter price
For a dance and a song.

So she ran again, looping and loping
Down the slope of discretion — to hide
(By then her mother had died)
As in a deadlocked wood — between pots and pans
Where now she stands (Where once her mother had stood)
Soothing and smoothing, burning her fingers
On little things

An unhandy woman, all thumbs,
Scrambling regret
On back burning rings.

Supplication Unanswered

i.m. Siege Moos, poet

This earth is not fit
For the meek
Or the timid
Or the gentle of heart

Till, at the last — the terrible, lasting last —
They kick

Heads averted
Like blind-folded donkeys
Kick over whole buckets
Of humiliation

All sweetness forgotten, immortally bitter
Gone over to death

And the world has to learn
To bear
Words
Singing such sweetness

To beg mercy
Of shadows

Treading the Wheel

Treading the wheel
Heart lacerated by grief
O my love, did we let the sharks have it?
Soul-eater shark, gilt-trimmed snout guzzling dross?
What merciful thumb, what cosmic fist, could redeem such
loss?
The Universe yawns, spawns waste upon waste — while we
Not even pawns
In a pawnless game
Face mortality
Without grace,

Lovers of truth, barely weaned off mother-earth's
                              fearful centricity
(We kiss the hem of your thought: Kant, Leibnitz, Descartes)
Sought eternity in the giving of stars
Willed God (Priests had nailed to a sprung double-cross)
Distilled from symmetry's immutable laws

Severing living from dead
And iron entered the soul, driven
Into a void's unbreathable hole
Tearing us too, o my love, for ever apart
Where nothing will testify
But the unforgiven hardness of heart.

Seduction

Homage to Jacques Offenbach, composer of 'The Tales of Hoffman'

A bleak house
A work house
A work to death house (Oh, the Victorians knew how
                                    to scewer their poor)
Though the interior now painted pale green — for Hope,
                                    flaking to uncertain azure

And, hopefully, we, nine, elderly, heart-bitten muses
Dance here to tinned, shredded tunes that embrace us
                                    like bemused boa constrictors
And, as we dance, stubby fingers grow slim, elegant even
Toes tip, swollen ankles raise arches:

    'Lass Dich nicht von Hoffman verführen .....'

Across golden-green rivers, the golden-green Mosel of
                                    the Alsace
Whence he came, our particular Orpheus, Hebraic envoy
                                    of light
To release us from wetness, deadness, arthritis and dark
With, in his hands, the rounded grapes of seduction:

    'Lass Dich nicht von Hoffman verführen, Hoffman
                                    verführen .....'

Shedding an age of dragons, death-adders, fly-traps
Oh, Jacques Offenbach, what a cruel century you were spared
You and your (Ungassed) Cantorial forebears
Who sang their soul out to God
— But you've come singing to us
So we may raise heavy feet in this East-End workhouse, built
To 'incalculate' the merciless virtue of work:

— 'Ha, you, you and you! Rub-a-dub-dub! Mr. Gradgrind
                                        wants you to scrub
And no spark in eye or smirk on mutinous lip!
Or out you go and you starve' —

But we lean on the soft cheek of this Orpheus' music

    'Lass Dich nicht von Hoffman verführen, Hoffman
                                        verführen .....'

Raise hands — not to serve or service, spool, tool or machine
But just — for the hell of it
For the hell of being nine elderly frumps
For the hell of no longer being in hell

Oh yes, let Hoffman come and seduce us, seduce us,
                                        seduce us .....

Hope

Hope wants to emigrate
Where to? Into whose
Worn-out, renegade shoes?

Hope, seeing red, buries head
In glorious Has-Been: eschews
Flat, dead, and confused
'Not-Yet'
— Alas, the transit-visa's been refused

Who now will hold the dialectical thread
Of spayed History going for dead?

— Hope changes address.

Tea for One

Into the house of the unattached lady
The afternoon enters on oily slicks
Through the foliage outside and the pot plants' long slings
On to the biscuits and assorted tea-things.

The youth with the milk, the baker, the biscuit-tin maker,
The breaker of flax for the linen serviettes,
The sugar-cane raker,
The pickers of tea, sick kids on their backs,
The girl in the laundry with itching red wrists,
The miller who sifts choking flour from grist:
All hitched, all pitched, into sweaty long shifts

Into the house of the unattached lady.
Time — like castor sugar — sifts
— And when the room grows dark
There's the bench in the park.

Lesser Evil

How much less is lesser?
How evil is less?
The weevils that crop these pastures of death
Are having a field-day, grow fat
Munch containment
                    BETTER THAN
When it comes to the crunch
Better than what?
Butter than guns?
Guns than nukes?
Nukes than ... what?

So, down we go at the deep end
Spluttering: 'Still, this isn't the end of the world'.
Wrong again!

To a Liberatress

(One who gave words to the wordless)

The long cord of patience
Plunges
Down to the deep
Where sleep
White enshelled tears
Where sand
Has entered the wound
Yet flowers
— Underneath towers of grinding stress —
Into lucent white spheres
And she who prizes
Such luminous loot
Rises
Bearing ripe fruit

Requiem for Two

If I should die, my love
Who will defend?
Bent over your spent life
As one would bend
Over a sweet spent shrub
If I should die
Who'll tend?

Yet if I lived
Short shrift
Will shift and dissipate
Your sweet song's gentle gift
Short shrift will cut adrift
The singer at the gate

If I should die
Who will reciprocate
The pity of your grave?

New Poems

Anatomy of Terror

Because we are not strong enough
We lean,
Because we lean
We are not strong enough.
Come, Mr. Clean, and take us by the scruff
Redeem! Redeem!
And if you are not clean
Just seem!

Because we are not straight enough
We dream
Of being pure and incorrupt
So that, on waking up,
We scream
For others' tainted, impure blood.

To Another Herald of Another Mourn

Little cock, why do you crow?
You made us oversleep
Five fathom deep
And your dancing and prancing
Makes us weep.

Little cock, who are your friends?
Is it the snazzy little black hen
That lays eggs for gentlemen
While we sleep
Leaving us with the chicken-feed.

Chirping trumpeter of the 'Crow-Slow'
Who sits on the fence, cooing 'Me-Too'
Who are you wooing?
Who's put the rings on your toe?
Who's put the clips on your wings?

Ark Without Covenant

To call it 'The People's Ark'
Was neat,
The bland misleading the blind
Meant to be left behind
To drown in our deceit.

But the raven's come back with an empty beak
The dove's lost its brief
Failing a single, green, hopeful leaf
The Ark may be springing a leak.

And here, cleaving the swallowing dark,
Comes the first ravenous shark.

Another Turn

The People's Prisons are empty
So are their stomachs
Hunger decrees:
'Jump at bait!'

Even at minnows, flaunted as sprats
Those who count the number of hooks
Will be silenced — for good.

The People's Prisons are empty, gape
This time, there'll be no reneging
No abjuration
— And no escape.

Avant-Garde 1938

(Seen from the big fossil of the Lawn Road flats, London NW3)

Let there be light!
Light into space!
This is no place to trace your name in gathered dust
No nest, reeking of late-Victorian bric-à-brac and must,
Feathered against the panic of the dispossessed
This is a tent
Flaps open to the steppes.

Bare, let all be bare!
Metal and stone, cold metal, porous stone
Walls painted flat,
Not meant to hold but to recede into thin air
Bold Bauhaus steel-flung chair in black
Not to lie prone but to spring back
In vigilance.
The enemy is everywhere. Beware
Of innocence!

Objects so rarefied and yet defined:
Stone jars — not paving stones
Where men, down on their hunkers, rattle bones —
Curved metal — not of prison bars.
Though walls are pale they still stand fast
The blast of bombs is coming from afar
— The planes have not yet passed:

Those who have fled this open paradise
To go and fight in Spain
Are killed. Or never seen again.
Or may come back like bridegrooms tricked, lips tight,
On whom and what, in misery and fright, was spilled.
This is the wound that must be licked.
— Defeat is the question where no answer lies.

Yet here — while Barclays Bank across the road
                                   still underwrites —
The draughty indoors flapping to the outdoors wind
In an unruly universe still to be cut to size
Still waiting to be disciplined.

After the Hurricane

After the hurricane
Owls grew unpopular
Had they not hooted their dismal 'To-whit'
Mightn't there still be blue skies?

So trees, cut down to size, uprooted,
Got rid of these croakers
Hurricane-gloaters
Brokers in blight

Who'll open the slit of their eyes
Only to night
Prefer to be blind
To the light.

Who gave them the right to be right?

After the hurricane
Owls found nowhere to hide.

1987

Avengers

Clusters of cunning, honeyless wasps,
They cling
To the bitter sting
Of their loss

They're the scabs left after the toss
Scratched and torn open at will
Reclaiming lust and power
— To kill

History is the twisted rope
Down which they clamber
To split, sunder and clamour
For blood — and no hope

The Blood of Others

(On being told that President Pinochet of Chile was coming to
the Birmingham International Exhibition — he did)

The blood of others — an entrance ticket (Maybe a truss?)
For bullet-proof necks
And here they strut
For us: their backers, their bankers, their claque.

Who are they, these connoisseurs of torturing hell?
Thugs come to the Fair.

Please, no fuss!
We prefer not to dwell
On things we sell (*)
Ploughshares aren't on offer
Ploughshares don't fill the barn or the Treasury's coffer
To keep these eminent pockets warm
We sell an innocuous sort of arm, rockets that
                                        never do any harm
Maybe, even a wee little you-know-what bomb
(Not our funeral! Not our tomb!)

Export in depth!
Murder at leisure!
The cries of those tortured to death
Pay no interest
Whatsoever.

* *Alan Clark, the then Trade Minister, advised representatives of
engineering companies planning to export equipment to Iraq, that
'the intended use of machines should be couched in such a manner
as to emphasize the peaceful aspect to which they will be put (The
Guardian, 14.5.91) — a few months before the Gulf War.*

Chip-Eaters

Eating from paperbags
Like sparrows
At bus stops,
Leaning against a wall
While the wind wraps yesterday's news round faded,
                                    mock-kuli jeans.

Pity them? Pity the ones who, willingly, killingly,
Have hooked days, weeks, years, to the tick-tock of mealtimes
Their life chopped small
Cud on the chopping-board, the unhumming drum,
                                    of humdrum existence

Who are hung with bells, set to ring, ring down, ring out,
Should they slither, snake, towards imagination ignited
With only the night to dip in — playing footsie with dreams

Who — like the mouse in the fairy-tale who ran through the
stew
(To improve the flavour) —
May never come out again
— Then, where was the cock that crowed?

Old women, grown 'wise', no longer serving as sauce
                                    (Over whose
meat?)
Whittled down — frugal as bone — to sparseness
Who were whistling the tune of freedom too soon
Woke up, called 'WITCHES', were turned into smoke
— Leaving no footprints

And yet ... and yet ...
Eating from paperbags
Elbows out, fingers picking, licking the unspeakable grease
Here, in this scruffy ill wind, is a whiff of the witches' brew,

Here is abundance: Take it! — Leave it! — Fly away, paper!
                                        — Go away, house! —
The greasy drumsticks; surrogate broomsticks of liberation.

Besides, these walls, they lean on
Will no longer support, no longer serve
As stalls for that cautiously nibbling domestic beast
Called wife, of this or that house.

Child's Equinox

My father, the sun
My mother, the moon
Have filled the shell of my ear
With the lilt of their song

I cannot yield
To the sun's cymbals of joy
I cannot shield
My mother's dark, fluted tears

Star-crossed by luminous spheres
A child eager to please
I breathe
Shadowy fears

Cosmology

When you make an infant smile
A star is dancing in the sky
But they who make a small child weep
Shall sleep as in a steaming sty.

Our vault of heaven hangs
Furling in these tiny hands
Spare the love and rot the child
And the cosmos will run wild

When a mother's loveless son
Shall asphyxiate our sun.

Decimation

*(At a war memorial in Itter, Tyrol, whose male population was
decimated at the 'Eastern Front')*

This is Hansl and Gretl country
The witch now sleeps in the till
When it tinkles she will
Gobble her fill
Remember?
Snap-Crackle-Kill

O Hansl, don't linger
Remember the finger
One finger in ten
Bit through
Though the ovens were lit — just then —
Not for you

Digging for Love

Adrift in pity for each other's need
They dig what love is left
Hip pities heaving hip
Giver, receiver, each
Of tendered, melancholy gift.

But then, a subtle shift
When, cleaving to a deeper seam,
They lift
And retrieve
An abandoned dream

As though
Within a narrowed rift
Life, love
Reprieved
Might flow again.

A Disease of the Heart

A disease of the heart
Grips the city
A disease of the heart
Spits on dreams

Mocks at pity
Whittles at definition
Till words grow brittle,
Can't hold, splinter into deceit

But the city fiddles and diddles,
Walls itself in
Round the old cow of gold.

Dirge for an Unconsuming Donkey

Why can't we make the donkey eat
Now we've safely tied his feet?
Monopoly has blocked the street
Duopoly has locked the gate
He can't escape
But all he does is scrimp and scrape.

We gave him all a donkey needs
Confound the beast! He just won't feed
Where is the whip? Where is the chain?
We can't stuff fodder down the drain.
Down on your knee! Consume! Consume!
Your abstinence is our doom.

Give him a bucket for to kick!
Quick! Step on it! The beast is sick.

'Too late. Too late', the donkey brayed
'Ten market forces won't revive.
The donkey lives you have betrayed
Monopoly! Duopoly! And even oligarchy,
                    squinting its crafty eyes.'
'Is that the price
To pay for asinine democracy?
It stinks on ice.'
          (Where donkeys are not meant to stray)

And thus he died.

Doctor A. Chekhov

—'Stay cold as ice!' —

Under his hands, the furnace-workers blew their final breath
The midnight babies crawled with lice
The typhus-stricken peasants fled to their huts and died

— 'Stay cold as ice!' —

His torn lungs bled, reeling his life towards a breathless death
And yet:
To weep here were to bend the healing knife

— 'Stay cold as ice!' —
What harsh, what sorrowful advice
Virulent doctor — distant, mocking friend.

The Empress of Hypothermia

The Empress of Hypothermia
Sits on an iron throne.
She withers flesh
She shivers bone
And when she unzips her bitter lips
Out come the writs for instant doom
And the one-bar fire will not be lit
And the coal will drown in the sealed-off pit
And death will sit in the flickering room

       Cold pillow under the head
       Cold hollow within the bed
       Feet furled at the frozen end of the world.
       The heart cannot hold.

The Empress of Hypothermia
Sits on a throne of gold.

Enclosures

After the enclosures: the fire,
After the people's land had been taken:
The burning haystacks, the manorhouse cindered,
So — up go the gallows
Ha-ho! Let fife, drum and musket stifle all cries! —

Now the turn of the cities:
The house of the poor sold over their body, over their head:
'Gung-ho', cry the respectable robbers:
           'Out with the scroungers!
           Out with the spongers!'
       And: 'We'll clear whole houses. No charge' —

And don't come us with foxes in holes, birds in their nests!
Not at a thousand grand a square foot.
Those who want, let them sleep in the street! Or go into service
There're plenty of dishes, there's plenty of dirt, to be scrubbed
                       by beggars
With up-turned palms
Between Chelsea and Wapping. Between Wapping and Chelsea
With rats, going up mahogany lifts, needing attention
Where excess drums on the swollen belly of glut
Where Our Lady of Profits washes immaculate hands in the
                      sewage of scandal.

       Sweet Thames, run filthy!

And we, you and I, where can we turn to still the trembling
               between finger and thumb?
Shall we stand, masterless sheep, bleating by DSS windows?
Have an 'S' (for scrounger) branded on our foreheads?
An 'F' (for fugitive) on our sons' chests, tenants of
                 cardboard boxes?
After the people's land had been stolen: the fires,
After enclosure: the burning haystacks.

       'Push Panic Button to Open' *

* *Seen on the door of a Kensington DSS office*

Endgame

The King and Queen of the castle
Sit on Heal's rattan chairs,
He oils the locks of his 12% stocks
She is the queen-bee of shares.
The parquet floor mirrors and sparkles,
Neutered Tom, that fastidious cat,
Who won't piss or shit on the carpet, only on
                              monogrammed mats,
Watches as the coffee machine hisses and drips,
                              drop by brown drop
Oh, if only the world would come to a stop
Here, at this neat little spot

                    To percolate
                    Immaculate.

But, in front of the gate, where the hungry dogs bark
'No, Maud, don't walk in the garden! It is getting too dark.
The riff-raff, the scum, have come for their share
To kidnap the knick-knacks we really can't spare
And tie us all up in a rocking-horse chair.' —

                    'I know how it feels',
                    Says the lady from Heal's

'But where, oh where, are the police, our friends,
Meant to defend
Civilization (as we know it) we represent?
Oh damn! Oh blow it! The thin blue line is getting too thin
Dial 999! — For Chris' sake, dial anywhere!' —
                    (Nemesis' wheel clicking into a snare)

There's nobody there - There's nobody there.

Feast in the City

The glittering diadems reflect the crystal chandelier
And every darling cleft — as white as Persil Automatic lye
                                        — lays bare

The precious stones De Beers
Extracted from Namibian bones.

                              Only connect.

Like penguins, tripping gravely in their long black tails,
Each guest has tracked and trails all others' current price.
Here 'smiles are sold' and 'looks are merchandise' *
That may compromise the facts, revealed in
                              the Financial Times.

                              Only connect.

But what's this, this shadow cast upon the soup
The waiter's heavy hands have scooped across
                              the elegantly tied white lies?
Oh drat! Oh gloomy fear! Black Africa has spat its wrath
Into the neo-post-imperial broth.

                              Only connect.

No, we won't meet murder on the way
It hides between the hidden hands
Bidding for 'Futures': Cocoa, Rubber, Lives
Un-futuring another hungry land.

                              Only connect

How should we weigh — and on which scale —
The starving bodies it will slay

* *See 'Hated Poverty' by Samuel Johnson*

Day after day, night after night
While mothers wail and priests have ceased to pray?

                                    Only connect.

A major mountebank will now address his guests
— From the flying trapeze of deception —
He won't connect. The needle of his eye contracts
Merely the ceremonious thread of malefaction.
The City's golden pillars — hollow in their truth —
Stand erect.

                            The tooth of History will
                            disconnect.

Gently, like Easing Hand into Glove

Gently, like easing hand into glove
We cast our vote through a slot. Meaning no harm
Ours no 'Shoot-to-Kill' arm. No Kingdom-Come shove
                                    towards the ultimate leap
(Why bother to pull the wool over the eyes of a sheep?)

In this, democracy's very own, booth,
Dove-less ark driven by sharks of the deep
Truth won't give suck at her atrophied tits
All we are given are slits. Vents
Kept ajar — that far, no further — by management

Provided, that is, we won't leap through this slotted reality
Go home and nuzzle at nullity:
Exemplary, oven-wise sheep.

Goodbye to all that

The glasses are dusty
Who here d'be drinking?
The tools have gone rusty
Whose hammer would knock?

I am thinking in circles
Precise but still shrinking
From whether or not ...
The 'Whole-Houses-Cleared' lot
Are trying the lock.

The Great Fear

This is the little prison
— Shut the gate! —
For which we've prayed.

We've scrimped and scraped
And have escaped
Behind this narrow, home-made gate..

How should we rate
Such knife-long thrift
Against the cataclysmic rift

Were gates to shift?
Were gates to gape?

Hung with the Glorious Rags

Hung with the glorious rags of inglorious defeat
The poor are unready to fight
Unwilling to win.

Trust? In spivs, straining poor people's tears
Through the sieve of their parenthetical grin?
Telling them what to mourn, when to grieve?

Tying the rope of deceit round their throat
The poor will choke
Dying of counterfeit hope.

Lost Generation

Having swallowed the stone of exile
Our elders viewed our still-smiling lips
                            With dismay.
They knew evil transcends. Will outstay.

And we, still given to the provisional,
Cannot reach those we wanted to spare:
                            Our unsmiling children.

Calypso: Island in the Sun

Remembering the glorious victory of the USA over the island of
Grenada

The backwater slaps against rotting moles.
Once there were pirates and dungeons up in the fort
Where now a barbed electrified wire circumscribes
A square of cement
Prisoners' feet may describe.

Tar has slagged the backwater's wharves
And sweetness, flower and fruit
Must come down — for a fist of cement — to the market
Where black-suited beetles, antennae chafing,
Circulate, sure of reward
Where a restless imperial power holds all the barbs in its hands.

The eye of the Mafia watches through the four watches of night,
Gives us this day our daily jab.
They who should guard us
Are part of the green smile of poison.

A small isle in the sun, of spice, has spluttered,
Has been snuffed out.
Once there were pirates and dungeons
Now a restless imperial power dances
Its hubris in pavementless streets.

The North-wind is pleading the Fifth Amendment.

Loot

(After Los Angeles heard the angels sing
— A lesson in applied economics)

Shopwindows are just a skin
Too thin
To keep the baddies out
To keep the goodies in.
Here's economics in full swing.

Here's economics on the rocks,
A tide, a torrent, skipping shares, tripping stocks
From WHOM? To WHOM?
To TOHU BOHU, sitting on top
Here's economics spitting LOOT.

— Don't shoot!

Not here *

Merciless death
looks out of all windows
                    Akhmatova

Not here
Here people pull curtains
Drawing a veil
Over what hurts them
The empty caverns to which they depart
Are of the heart

* *Translation of the Russian 'U Nas'*

Musician

i.m. Hans Eisler who was ordered to 'compose' a national anthem for the GDR — and did

In the echoing depths of his being
He hears the poor, thrumming their fugue of defeat,
Hears the thud of their feet eternally fleeing.
The beating of beaten hearts
Beats through his brazen art
Not of harps — but of drums,
But of trumpets at sharpest sharp.

Surfacing from such deep-shaft work,
He'd smirk, poke fun at his sob-sister heart,
Play the macho's part: 'Real hard',
Unsnarl the blast of bone-splintering trombones
Into arpeggios; nosegays of thistles, falling apart.

Yet, hearing his martial art trumpeted in a murderous world,
Tears at membranes he thought had scarred
Not to be vetted for intellectual pride,
Furls to half-mast position
Claims links with an authorized past,
Over-subscribes to a hallowed tradition
Of hymns, tra-la-la's, this or that old warlike march:
Thump! Thump! Thump! Let them jump to the pitch
Of radical Kitsch!

Threatened by powerful scribes
Promises earnest revision.
Back-slides. Denies. Lies.
Drinks
And, at long last, shrinks
Back to the business in hand:
To listen. To understand. To sing and lament.

The Sour Tale of Poor B.B.,
the Vinegar-Man

B.B., the Vinegar-Man, saw fit to cleanse the head of man
                              from louse and nit and other vermin
So off he ran into the street, beat Pegasus
                              (Horse with three feet) and cried:
'Here's vinegar, the acid test, to be applied against cloying pest
'Sugar and spice are for blind mice. My medicine may make
                    you spit but lets the scabs fall from your eyes.
'Get rid of nits!   Nits will be lice
'(As Cromwell realized whose head itched twice
                              when excavated from the pits).'

Alas, where was this acid test, applied to poor B.B.'s own head
When, in one nest with parasites, he justified
                              their bloody rule of thumb?
'Why', cried this canny Machiavel, 'leave all the worst tricks
                              to the hounds of Hell?
'He who delouses last, had better delouse well.'

This cure — spoonfed on iron spoon — held no allurement
                              to the poor, innured in want.
Along the avenues of bliss to come, they picked up stones,
                              they picked up sticks,
Out of the slums flew building-bricks,
Spilled acid between B.B.'s lips and song
                              (or rather between whip and thong)
Hurting poor B.B. to the quick.
Who here was trickster, who was tricked?   Who conned?
He died in nineteen fifty-six.

A Poor, Young Immigrant's London

*(After coming across a demonstration of Turkish workers
celebrating May 1st in Stoke Newington High Street)*

Tottenham Court Road, station of my cross
Going north to Camden to doss
Going east to Hackney to be gypped by the boss
But opening my lips to sing
When the demo marches to Newington Green.

Between Holborn and Mornington Crescent
Past the bared fangs of vertical slums
I've spilled the have-beens of my confessions,
Going at it, hammer and too-loose tongue,
Cracking dialectical nuts that can't be undone
— And still am young.

                But, on the long and painful run
                From where I was born
                My heart has been torn.

O Hackney, where they knee my groin,
Handing out Friday's miserly coin
Humbling me, not once or twice, but for the rest of my life
Pulling the wool over an illegal immigrant's eyes
About an illegal immigrant's price.

                If only, if only, Barclays Bank
                Would be my friend!

O London stones! O London stones!
Where every step is warning my bones:
                        against the threat of tomorrow.
Ah! Lucky Macbeth! — Tomorrow may bring
                          deportation to death
— 'Well, we may give you another week!'
                            — make the pips squeak.

In this country that once seemed so free
Alas, alack, the pip is me.

O pimp-run stews round King's X Station!
                    Round dirty, sinful Paddington Green!
Where I mustn't go. Where I've never been.
Father and mother's eyes would view such transgression
Across thousands of miles of hurt expression,
Reject the reject who fled with dreams to burn
Who left them, weak with weeping, with nowhere to turn

A brideless, loveless, footloose bum,
Tottenham Court Road, here I come.

The Poet Who Sings Below Stairs

i.m. Howard Mingham, poet, 1952-1984

The poet who sings below stairs
Hears the voice of the master.
The poet who lives on sweet airs
Is courting disaster.

Turning his innermost shirt
He'll get hurt, burnt to the skin.
The poet who waits below stairs
Must learn to work faster.

O Marjory Daw, riding so tall,
Here is no see-saw, with you bestriding the top
But a small cage-bird's teetering swing
And the harder they fall the sweeter they sing.

O Marjory Daw, why don't you drop
A sop of love down your carpeted stairs
To the poet below
Before he despairs.

P.M.

(Post mortem 1992)

Since our ears are shallow
(Though our beaks non-stop)
Who listens to the nightingale?
We listen to the frog.

Have we run out of weasel-words
To ease us off the hook?
Who listens to the nightingale?
We listen to the rook.

And, warbling with vox populi,
Set up a tinny squawk.
Who listens to the nightingale
While our betters talk?

We do not sing — but, dry-tongued, cheep
Like mummers at the door,
Are waiting for the vultures' leap
— As we have done before.

Ripeness is All

An affable man, he treasures
His maturity's hard-nosed acts.
'What did you expect?' is the text
Round which he gathers
His measured, incontrovertible facts.

'Feather your nest while you may!
When it comes down to brass-tacks
A dividend, due at the ripened year's end,
Is a man's very best friend.

Best not to dissent!'

Pornography

On being shown the naked body of his mother (murdered by special request), Nero said: 'Not bad!'

                                     The Sun, Rome, A.D. 59

'The centre cannot hold'
How bloody true!
Except: the circus wheel, periphery on which we ride so

                                     merrily
Now shrinks and — verily, verily — stinks too.

Where eyes daren't see
Where brains daren't think
Save in conformity with the enormity
— Panopticum of lies —
That twist and have to be undone
Before we can begin to live or even to exist
Something, not very brave, not very bold
Will give.

The centre that can't hold now sinks
Into a mouldy lust, a lusty mould,
Doused with the stinks of cruelty and dung.
Ha-Ho! What fun!
Across the thrash-hold of the torturer's tongs.

The Smile

*On seeing an old photograph of Thomas Mann smiling at Attila
Joseph. Thomas Mann was, of course, Thomas Mann. Attila
Joseph was a Hungarian poet of genius who died young and
hungry.*

The best suit
The good suit
The only suit

— Smile please!

Apart from the honour
Was there some — was there any —
Promise to be snatched as it were
From mid-air?

Run out of fat, the frying-pan shilly-shallies
While the door, sullen with winter,
Refuses to close
Stuck in the status quo.

The mattress, springless as straw,
Nuzzles the floor-boards,
Straw — bride of his dreams —
On the pig farm back home.

Apart from the honour
Was there some ... any ...
On the nod as it were?

Hooked to the door
The best suit
The only suit
Dangles

Still, that was a nice smile.

True Prophets

To have to repeat, again and again,
What, leaning on History's prompting propelling wing,
                                 has been proven,
To chew — suppressing hiccups of contradictions
                          — the ever correct conclusions
Dangling like noodles from lips that have split
                            (Truth-sayers' affliction),
To nail — like incompetent smiths — the red-hot iron of truth
To the kicking hoof of illusion, delusion

      AND FAIL

By the old runnel they sit,
Funnel, from the original crystal spring
Precious aged wine into vessels they'll rinse free
                        of two-tongued confusion.
Why is it nobody drinks?
Has the wine grown too old?
Their voices too cold to convince?
Or are they waiting for the hard-of-hearing, harder-of-heart
To depart, grow extinct?

Tinnitus of Love

—'That noise! Can't you hear it? Like the hissing of steam.'—
Torn from a dream, I strain, rally to lie:
'Oh yes, I can hear it: like the hissing of steam
Or a train rushing by.' —

Lying alone, I, too, can now hear it:
The hissing of steam
A train rushing by
Though there's no one with whom to share it:
Love or white lie?

Unanchored Beds

'Unanchored beds are dangerous'
                    The Governor of Feltham Remand Centre

'Unanchored beds are dangerous'
Why? Just tell us — why!
Will they take off, like carnivorous bats, and fly
Into a prisonless sky?

Or, risen vertically
Tight — oh, so tight! — under the chin,
Give felons the right
To do themselves in?

Nail them down! Nail them down, these noctiverous pests!
We don't allow Walpurgis-nights among our guests.
Four dangling youngsters in a row
And how many others still to go?

Budget permitting
We'll do some re-fitting.

Vital Statistics

What is the unit for measuring truth and integrity?
Can they be bought and sold in the market?
Under or over the counter?
What is their price, given how many degrees of pressure?
Devalued, tell us the rate of deflation!
Going up? Going down? With, at the back,
Lip-service provided?
— Statisticians will sing — even as birds being trussed.

Virgin Aunt in the Family's Way

We pay her the shell of respect.

Like a ship in a bottle
Trim, ship-shape, decked out in fine fettle
She's ready to cleave, to plough her own trail.
Yet she never will leave. (Where would she go?)
Never will fill the void of her sail,

Not having found — nor having lost —
Her East or her West
Unhitched to stars, untossed by seas
Sealed-in yet bare
Ship eclipsed within ship under a curving glass
Here and there streaked with feathery dust
(As weals will crust unhealing scars)
Thus auntie, furling herself to herself.

Those were clever fingers
That put her up on the shelf.

Virgin Death

First singly, one by one,
Her lovers died
Then as though on the run
None would be left behind

She lies in bed
Still as a stone
Whom all have fled
To die alone

The Weaning

They adore me
Dancing before me the timid steps of blind-man's buff
And I shall sink — oh, let me sink! —
Into the cat's cradle of hugs,
Drink in the flood
Of milk-white love.
Never enough! Never enough!
Soon spent. Soon spilt.
When clenched, like frightened fists
They will resent my tendered lips
Repent
The kisses
Kissed.

And I
Unfledged before this seeping frost
Unquenched in love's eclipse
Will have forgotten
What I lost
No longer miss

Shall kill

Old People's Home

Now the bird has been caught
Now the net's been drawn tight
Four narrow walls
And nowhere to hide.

This is the ice floe
That will float you to death
Learn to say 'Thank you'
Under your breath.

Why the Sparrow is Cocking his Head

As a pensioned-off crook
Might still crook his fingers
As though fingering the locks he once sprang,

Sparrow — né Robin — throat long gone bloated and dumb —
Is cocking his head, always cocking his head,
As though lending an ear to the songs he once sang.

But now all is circumspect chirping and cheeping
Wanting the resonance (Oh, song of my heart!)
Of the pipe dream. The dream-pipe broken.

Ah, but Sparrow too has his dreams:
To rise — a songless lark —
Into the blue, the commanding, heights

Where the sparrow-hawks wait
Where little feathers will fly.
And again, once again

The birds of the sky, a-sighing and a-sobbing
Will weep for one who'll never again, never again
Be Cock Robin

Who sang.

Giant Thaw

He stirs. Sighs. Weeping, his eyes
Drown forests of untold fears
Leaping over the frozen locks of petrified lies.
He hears

How many tides of pain
Have been spilled
To soften such snow.
Shall we ever again, after such frost,
— Even tossed into the green hammock of spring —
Dare letting go?

Those who were killed or lost
Cling — reprieved as with hooks —
To shifting floes drifting apart.
Let the juddering snow-ploughs retrieve
Let them thaw
Our shuddering heart.

September Morning

Tree in front of the window
Unspeckled, unfreckled, all green

    In between

A timid sun picking its way
Till the grey spattering rainclouds arrive.
I'm still alive
A little later each day.

You may stand down now

The souls of the dead are driven
To seek the warmth of living love.
Not given to giving, we've hidden
Our inadequate hearts.

Having killed the dove, sweet bird of innocence,
With more than one stone
How can we atone
Riven by guilt and wilful impenitence?

And when - for somewhere to lay our head
We turn to the dead in their rubble of bone
We're driven, unshriven and unforgiven,
Against the rock of lipless oblivion.

Forgetting - we are forgot.

Christian Duty

Forgive thy enemy
If you can spare the breath.
Forgive the enemy of the poor
You condemn them to death.
The kiss of the shark
Will be all they have left.

Post-Mural Liberators

Any old dreams for sale?
Soiled dogma? Spoiled expectations?
We'll buy up the lot
For the old, bloodied, rag-and-bone shop.

Any old chains to mend?
To bend? Making amends
For short means, long ends?
Repent! — Repent of being not sufficiently innocent!

Turn, you turnkeys of the wall!
Padlocked before, and deadlocked after, fall.
Given Freedom's small change
You'll be the free-running chicken on our range.

We are merchants of guilt.
The sweet milk of freedom you spurned and spilled
Has turned — to churn our swill
— We still know how to kill.

Prospect of Fire

This smallish bag of blood and slime
Will, in its own good, own bad, time
— Wild atoms torn along new lines —
Revert to ashes.

A bird of evanescent form
The preening Phoenix of re-hashes
Knows how to pirouette upon a pyre
And, pirouetting,
Be reborn

In fire.

Two Poets

Marina Tvetskayava listens to Mayakovski reading his poems in the Café Voltaire, in Paris — two years before his, fourteen years before her, suicide.

One knows
Oh, one knows

      Bears are meant to dance
      Bears are licensed to prance
      With abundance — as though they were free
      And, given a chance to cut loose
      — Even driven to flee —
      They may choose
      Not to run
      They have swallowed the noose

One knows
Oh, one knows

      Riven by grief, by despair
      At what they themselves helped to loose
      They'll set foot before foot
      Even lame
      Breathe fire
      As though there still was the air
      To fan — or kindle — a flame

Then go home to die in their lair

What has been given

What has been given
May be ungiven
And those driven
Into exile and death
Will not come back

Will not return
When carnage, turning its bloody coat,
Learns the language of freedom
By rote.

Must we earn
The right
To fight
For free breath?

Must we learn
Not to burn
Our own flesh?

Fraternal Critic

Here comes the woodpecker.
It pecks wood.
It doesn't always peck wood,
Actually, mostly, it doesn't

But when it does — look out birds!
What pecking and picking!
— 'See this? — That's the way to peck wood.' —
The birds sit and consider.
The woodpecker is a very thin bird.

Lot's Children

Their eyes strain back
Back to the evil they've seen though blind.
There was nowhere to hide.
Where were the Seraphim to guide away from putrefaction?
Besides, up to the night they burned
                              — burst crimson fruit of fire —
Both Sodom and Gommorah did all right
With City-Shares to climb right through the last evasive action
— As though the slime might yet cement and bind.

Whose were the lies?
It would appear God's mills no longer grind
But kill in pyramidal pyres, blind to redemption,
That spit into the raging skies.

They who had fled
Have eyes too sharply etched
To comprehend their near-exemption
And will avert their gaze from dreams of gentler days
That might contend
Where now they dwell:
The outer suburbs of accustomed hell.

The Great Tilting

Smugglers, who are boating illegal immigrants from Morocco to Gibraltar and from Turkey to Greece, have taken to decanting their cargos half way across the sea.

We tilt the plate to share the bread
With those we mean to live.
Let others tilt their dead-end boat
To make blind hunger's cargo float
Away from any land.

The tilters — Godfather Europe's new-found friends —
Let them contend with wild starvation's gap-mouth load
Leaving death's invoice on some lonely strand,
Mouths eating sand,

And if their bodies will not sink but float
Upstream where rivers cannot hold and burst,
This our continent, incontinent on its exclusive pot of gold,
May — growing rank — begin to stink,
Dying, it too, of hunger and of thirst

— Before we can repent.

On Being Given a Stone

Futureless present, ripped off blasted past
A stone miscast
From first to last

Chipped off 'The Wall', gift-wrapped, trapped into shiny box
Paid for in blood. Now sold
A ghoulish, a macabre hoax

To reassure superior blokes
That what they did was right
Not wrong

While hate and spite still write on the last refuge of the dead;
— 'Out with the Yids!' — *
Here's tyranny TRANSFIXED. Not overcome.

Here's Liberty - without the bread -
A stony crumb.

* *For instance, on the tombstone in East Berlin of Bertold*
Brecht who was not a Jew.

Come-Down

Were I to sleep on barren desert sands
Fingered by lingering moon and star
Would I be raised — an inverse avatar —
To the ethereal vaulting sky
Above the dross, the treadmill fear
I must bestride — of loss?

Were I to lie on desert sands
How I should toss, straining to hear
The soft crunch of my cattle's feet.
My camels munch the cud-end of their sleep
Oh, I should weep most uncelestial tears
For every straying sheep, each lost lamb's bleat

And lie
Blind to the moon, the stars, the sky
Dagger in hand
To apprehend, defy and brave
Each fleeting shadow creeping by
Not freed but — fearfully — enslaved
To human need.

To the Professors of Bad Faith

New wisdom drips
Too trippingly
From lips
Gone newly stiff.

They'd call a spade a shovel
And the noose a dialectical twist
Would lick and trick and grovel
Spit on the bloody dead,
Now say they were misled.

The same old knavish fools
Who say they were misled,
Spools long run out of thread,
Now clamour for new tools
Slide-rules for sliding truth:

'History's cruel rules
No longer fit. Are too uncouth
Dilute! Dilute! Dilute!
Or, better still, omit!' —

And in an unclenched fist
Some ancient muddled dope
— Bold as a new-washed brain
Cold as the bodies that (regrettably) were slain —
Is offered up again

And will be sold — who knows?
— New lies for old —
As riddled, griddled, expurgated, hope
— For which we yearn
For which we thirst.

They Came Back

They came back from the land of their furthermost hope
Like snowmen shrunk
Yet boding no sun but frozen dread,
Came back like diamonds splintered; toads, jewel torn
                                        from their head
Were 'unmasked' as 'Poisoners of the People's Bread'
Coming back from the land of the untold dead.

Yet, when the truth did burst through
                            — like a blood-spattered groom
Rising from the tent where the bride, no longer festooned,
Lay awaiting her doom —
Who now will pay these spillers of bloody news the debt
For the unbreathable years, fears closing in like an iron net
That would deny, that would belie, the untold dead?

Executioners (who die in their bed)
Do not visit their victims' tomb,
The pick-axe does not regret
Nor retract
While the earth, that old black pudding, still steams
With our brothers' murdered dreams.

Stone Gods

(After seeing the exhibition 'The Art of Ancient Mexico')

Stone gods
Will not forgive   Nor give
Nor, being incarnate,   Need be reborn.
Even the stone-She,   gripping swollen tits in swollen fists
            Will be — no silky, milky, heart-fed sap —
            Torn open   And sucked dry.
                    There is no joy.

Do not expect   But what's already known
All ends are dead   Precluding chance
                    And hope.

But if the god of wind should dance before,
                            and tender his big snout,
            To the untender gods of rain
Such mercy, to be wrenchingly reborn, has to be honed
                    By sacrifice

                    Heart-torn.

Remembering Jack

Remembering Jack
Who drank (Or so we're told)
Who'd spank his boys
And beat his wife
In front of the kids' frightened eyes.

Remembering Jack
Who loved James Joyce
Who shared his crummy mews
And dumpling stews
Who'd read all Proust
And called his cat 'Old Oedipoos'.

Remembering Jack
Who was found dead
In someone's loo,
Who left his wife without a sou
(Or so we're told)
The second wife was rich and fat
(But I am old and I forget)

Remembering Jack
With whom we spent
Five windward years of our youth,
Remembering Jack
A good and kind and gentle friend.

TELL US THE TRUTH!

Session with an Unwilling Guest
or
The Impossibility of Discourse between Unequals

This owl sits in resentment's cage
Head tucked into ruff — as for protective custody
(Its ev'ry movement mimes escape)
Claws twist in silent rage
At rays of light that would unhood the eyes
As though to paralyse the will to flight

Into a soothing, lightless night
Where owl would spike, eat and regurgitate defenceless mice
Not being fed dead things the creature on the other side
Provides: False friend who's lost, or hides, its wings
Clings while it pries, denies
The nearness that divides

And cries

Roll-Call

For the fallen of both sides, 1983

'Conqueror'
'Tigerfish', 'Seawolf' and 'Dart'
What rattling names!
But the men who went down
Or burnt in the flames
Were just Jimmy or Juan or James

Who pushed them down?
Who stopped their heart
'Tigerfish', 'Seawolf' or 'Dart'
Or was it some speculating shark
Hiding its game?

What a shame
Jimmy and Juan and James
Went down in the dark,
Not knowing the name of the game.

Spring — War Laying Its Eggs

How would you like a textbook operation?
Remove your brain and march on chopped-off feet!
The stumps of your two hands disintegrating
Might still come handy for some cerebration,
Surrendering the twice-cleft bits still left.
        On wings no turkey-shoot would care to fly
             the headless birds are gliding by.

A poisoned war needs poisoned tools.
The gentlemen — no fools — who mean the means
(Though not particular about the ends)
Who clinched their dirty deals with dirty hands
Now prune their roses far from killing-fields
In England's green and pleasant land,
Say: Surrey, Middlesex and Kent.
        On wings no turkey-shoot would care to fly
             the headless birds are gliding by.

Demand calls for supply and slaughter fills the bill.
The way to live is to let others die
Or, better still,
Supply those bastards with the means to kill.
        On wings no turkey-shoot would care to fly
             the headless birds are gliding by.

Unsummoned by Bells

The Sunday-Afternoon-Man
Walks the dog through the cold,
The Sunday-Afternoon-Man
Halts where he is towed.

The dog splashes a wintry message
Against a Telecom tree.
At home, the missis mashes
Afternoon teabag tea.

        And is there honey still for tea
        The way it's always been?
        And waits dear Alice still by the gate
        To have a look at the Queen?

But look! Oh see!
Here's the muffin-man, the nuffin-man,
Ringing his bell through the pea-soup green,
From the cage of his bones.

        And sits the Empire still on its throne
        To dilly-dally its loyal subjects on its knee
        The way it's been before?
        And do the church bells ding-dong-ding
        Straight from the churchyard door?

        O hand in glove!
        O glove in hand!
        You've turned to gravel, mud and sand

But look! O see!
Here sits the telly, will shilly-shally
The straight and the narrow
And wheedle, through the eye of a needle,
The rich with the poor

And send us to sleep
To the Kingdom of Snore.

While the burglar-alarm
Below the stairs
Sings inconsolate airs,
But nobody cares

Nobody cares.

Who was the Child?

Who was the child
That cried:
'The Emperor's got no clothes'?

An awkward kid,
Sties in both eyes,
A snotty nose,

They beat it up
As soon as they got it home,
Alone. *

* Present abode unknown.

To a Poet at the End of an Era

Yes, this is our circumscribed small life.   Why maul it?
Lying in wait for our flawed excuses, off-white lies,
And in the name of what rebellious God (You would not
recognize)
More deeply bruise it?

Yes, the mirror in the upstairs tomb averts its face,
The wedded bed is tepid as a tap that drips on ice,
But in the name of what abiding grace, which overflowing
Cupid,
Still traduce it?

Yes, our slotted life has clotted between clocking-in and late-
night news,
But in the name of which vindictive, mocking god (You would
despise)
Reach for the knife?

Bark while stocks last?
Poet, we shall not last

And nor will you.

Reversal Reversed

Hooked in the morning
    Nemesis' warning
Rooked in the night
    Black Furies' delight

When the red bull of despair
    Will tear
Through the hoodwinking air

And a shrill tocsin rings in
    Not that devious 'Vision Thing' *
But the raw howl of rioting

And those who stole our bread
    Will eat dread

February 1993

---

* *Expression used, derogatively, by a former President of the US and subsequently politicians nearer home, to distance themselves from the superfluous burden of 'ideas' - an old ploy to smuggle in unnamed ideas of their own.*

Art of Friendship

As friendship ripens
We dis-spell the spiel of lies:
— 'Oh no' — 'Not yet' — 'Not quite' —
We hid behind.
Will the new, truer, darker light
Unbind the bonds
We have so fondly tied?

Rocks, ravines, drop below each life.
Who wants to dive
Down to the bearded sisters as they spin and plot
While surfaces seem innocently bright?
Can we devise a knot that ties
Yet will unknot the I's?
We were? Are not?